How to Help Yourself With Self-Help

A Short Guide on How to Use Self-Help Books to Achieve Your Goals

By Martin Meadows

Download Another Book for Free

I want to thank you for buying my book and offer you another book (just as valuable as this one): *Grit: How to Keep Going When You Want to Give Up*, completely free.

Visit the link below to receive it:

https://www.profoundselfimprovement.com/selfhelp

In *Grit*, I'll tell you exactly how to stick to your goals, using proven methods from peak performers and science.

In addition to getting *Grit*, you'll also have an opportunity to get my new books for free, enter giveaways, and receive other valuable emails from me.

Again, here's the link to sign up:

https://www.profoundselfimprovement.com/selfhelp

Table of Contents

Prologue

Self-help is useless.

Self-help is life-changing.

These two opinions are diametrically different, yet both can be equally true.

What makes the difference between those who help themselves with self-help and those who are disappointed by it?

In this book, I intend to answer this question and offer some pointers on how to learn more effectively from self-help books.

It might sound strange coming from a self-help author, but the reason why I decided to write this book grew out of my frustration with the industry. The world of self-help has a lot of traps, and throughout the years, I've fallen into probably all of them.

Despite this, if it weren't for self-help books, I would have never accomplished most, if any, of the goals that I've managed to reach. When approached the right way, self-improvement books can help you get real-world results, and not just ephemeral bursts of useless motivation.

In *How to Help Yourself With Self-Help*, I want to share with you my observations and personal experiences, in hopes that you too can use self-help to reach your goals and enjoy continuous personal growth.

I don't expect you to implement everything from this book. Think of it as a toolbox. Pick whatever you need for the specific task at hand. If the tool doesn't work, discard it and try something else.

This is not a philosophical book, and it's short for a reason. I just want to show you the traps and teach you how to avoid them. I'll give you the tools that it takes to fully utilize self-help and encourage you to try them out so you can become your own coach. Our goal is consistent action, not consistent reading.

Are you ready to hear more? If so, let's turn the page and explore the five most common pitfalls of self-help and how to avoid them.

Chapter 1: Avoid the 5 Most Common Self-Help Pitfalls

When you familiarize yourself with the common pitfalls of self-help and learn how to avoid them, you'll be well on your way to getting real-world results.

This is the longest chapter in this book because these mistakes and traps have the most significant impact on your results. Let's discuss these dangers and learn how to avoid them.

1. Reading Without Taking Action

Unlike many other book genres, the chief reason why people read self-help is because they want to solve a specific problem in their lives. Of course, you can read this genre out of curiosity, but if you're reading a self-help book, you're probably looking for real-world results and not just reading for the sake of reading.

This leads us to the biggest trap of self-help: reading without taking action.

Think of the last few self-help titles you've read. What advice did you implement from them? What changes did you make in your life based on the information you got from reading?

If you read them specifically to improve yourself yet did nothing upon finishing them, you wasted your time. For all intents and purposes, you might have spent a few hours lying in a hammock and it would have been just as useful for your goals.

Don't get me wrong: I fall victim to this, too. I've read dozens, if not hundreds, of self-help books and have acted only on a small portion of them.

Of course, it's unrealistic to assume that every book will have an impact on your life. We aren't aiming for perfection. The goal is simply to increase the percentage of books that produce real-world results for us. And for that, we can—and should—become more selective with our reading in the following ways:

1. Address your current biggest pain—There are countless problems you can solve with self-help books. However, if the problem you're trying to fix is only a minor inconvenience, you'll be less pressed to implement advice than if it were a big, burning problem with a more severe impact on your life. What issues keep you up at night? What worries or challenges are on your mind most frequently? Which books could help you address them?

2. Look for actual, real-world how-to information—Many narrative non-fiction books provide an entertaining read, but they don't always offer particularly actionable advice. For this reason, I'm partial to traditional "here's how you do it" books that deliver clear-cut advice. For the same reason, it's best to stay away from "inspirational" books that might give you a temporary boost of motivation but don't offer practical advice to help you instigate permanent change.

3. Find simple advice—If you can't easily tell what the book is about, or upon finishing it, you have no idea what the fundamental concepts were, you won't learn effectively from it. If you're confused about how to get started, you most likely won't start at all. A good self-help book should strive for simplicity and offer clearly laid out key concepts everyone can act on.

As a quick exercise, open the last self-help book you've read that meets these requirements. Now find a single piece of advice to implement today. If you make it a habit—and I'm not asking for much, just one single tip to follow—you'll dramatically increase the value you get out of self-help.

2. Following the Wrong People

One of the best things about self-help is that everyone can write it, which is good, because the more perspectives there are, the higher the odds of finding someone with whom you resonate. On the other hand, one of the worst things about self-help is that since you don't need any qualifications to write self-help, everyone can do it.

And that's where the problem lies: what constitutes the right "qualifications" or makes a self-help author credible?

Is it a formal education? A large body of work? A nice author picture? A foreword written by a celebrity?

I'd argue that what makes someone credible to write self-help is personal experience, ideally combined with a deep understanding of their audience.

Your best friend doesn't need to hold a master's degree in psychology to give you useful advice. If they know you well, and you know them well, you trust their judgment—particularly if they've dealt with the same challenges you have. More often than not, you'd rather act on their advice than on the advice you'd get from a professor of psychology.

That's why I like to select the authors I read as if I were looking for a friend. If I stumble upon a book that might be useful to me but I'm unfamiliar with its author, I download a free sample and then look for the following things:

1. Make sure they're imperfect—As counterintuitive as it sounds, the authors who are most vulnerable and open about their failures are the most trustworthy.

We imperfect humans find it hard to resonate with perfect people, so if the author paints themselves as such, how likely are you to treat their advice seriously? If you can't see yourself in the author you're reading, you won't act on their advice. In the same way, all of our friends have flaws, as it's difficult to have a deep connection with a seemingly perfect person.

For this reason, I stay away from any author who appears to be too perfect: who claims to know all the answers, who has never failed, or who talks from a position of authority in that annoying way your most despised high school teacher did.

2. Make sure they share your core values— This may require you to read between the lines, but it's usually possible to identify the author's values even if they don't talk about them outright. Likewise, during a brief conversation with a stranger, based not only on what they say but also on their body language, it's fairly easy to get a rough idea of who they are.

If there's a mismatch between your core values and the values of the author you're reading, it's unlikely they'll push the right buttons to get you to take action. You can be friends with a person with opposite beliefs, but if you differ at the level of fundamental core values, it's unlikely you would ever have a close connection with them.

Personally, as much as I enjoy being productive, I don't resonate with writers whose core values revolve around work at the expense of everything else. You know the type: they talk about the never-ending hustle, sacrifices, and busy schedules.

I don't feel compelled to act on their advice because I don't want to be like them. That's not to say that people who espouse these ideas are wrong. Their life philosophy might resonate with you, but it doesn't align with my values. Instead, I prefer authors who prioritize smart work, efficiency and balance in life, and whose writing style is peaceful and understanding rather than violent and frantic.

Age, gender, religion, location, and a host of other factors can also affect how effective an author will be at inspiring you to take action.

For example, if you're a Christian and religion is vital to you, then Christian self-help authors might resonate with you more than non-Christian authors. On the other hand, the words of a Christian self-help author will most likely fall on deaf ears when read by an atheist.

What are you looking for in a friend? Which authors share these characteristics and would be most likely to inspire you to take action?

3. Make sure they practice what they preach— I like to see examples of the author following the principles they share, learning from their mistakes, dealing with obstacles, and failing their way to success.

A book of inspirational platitudes that's filled with repetitive stories depicting other people but lacking in any examples of personal experience from the author is unlikely to convince you to take action.

Self-help is a subjective, highly personal genre where the author's experience—not just the experiences of the people they portray—plays a significant role. We learn best through stories: make sure the authors you follow teach you through their own stories, too.

3. Seeking Secrets

Humans have an affinity for magic potions, wonder drugs, quick fixes, and silver bullets. We all know that these don't exist, but that doesn't prevent many self-help readers from trolling the bestseller lists in search of that one final secret they need to change their lives.

I know because I used to do that, too. I was constantly looking for something that would be the key to changing my world. If I couldn't find it in this book, then surely I would find it in that one. Oh, it's not there either? Then this book right over here must have the secret answers.

Of course, it's not just readers who are guilty of this. This problem exists primarily because of authors and publishing companies promising more than they can give. According to them, you can't sell a book that tells it like it is. A bestseller needs to provide revolutionary advice— something fresh and unique, the missing piece that will change your life overnight—even if it's all smoke and mirrors.

In reality, no book will magically transform your life. Despite their beautiful packaging and easy to remember acronyms, the "secrets" taught in books don't guarantee anything. They come from authors' trials, failures, mistakes, frustrations, and finally, successes, because in the end, all self-help advice is subjective and doesn't necessarily work for everyone.

As a self-help author, I would love to share exclusive secrets with my readers that will transform their entire lives overnight. But the truth is that you produce 99% of results (my highly *unscientific* estimate) by following a few fundamental principles.

For example, each year hundreds of new fitness books hit the market. They all come with revolutionary, unique spins on the topic, but the truth is that none of them contain secrets that will magically make you fit. No matter how many of these books you read, you'll eventually realize that getting in shape has nothing to do with exotic supplements, unusual exercises, or innovative fitness equipment.

The fundamentals that you probably already know well are what matters; the rest is like an icing on the cake. You should find an exercise that you enjoy that works out your entire body. Work out to put your body under more and more stress to build muscle. Eat whole foods and stay away from processed junk. Do these things consistently over and over again, tweaking things based on your results.

You know all of this already. Sure, it doesn't have the same allure as a revolutionary method that scientists claim will boost your fat loss by 495%, but our bodies haven't changed much in thousands of years. People were fit a hundred years ago, in the medieval period, in ancient Greece, and in any other period of history—and none of them needed today's "secrets."

Of course, the devil is in the details, but this largely comes down to a trial and error process. Books can give you pointers how to deal with particular challenges, but this more detailed knowledge should come later, *after* you implement the fundamentals that you can best learn from evergreen, non-gimmicky bestsellers.

In most areas of life, the purported secrets might give you an additional edge, but they mean nothing if you don't do the most important things first. Seeking that one secret is a waste of time if the foundation is lacking. Imagine going to a hardware store, trying dozens of different hammers to find the one that has a magical grip that drives nails by itself. It's preposterous to think that such a thing exists, yet it's not that different from the behavior of people who read one self-help book after another to find that one magical secret without doing much else.

To avoid this pitfall, be skeptical when you encounter promises of incredible secrets. More often than not, the only miraculous results they produce are increased book sales for the author. Instead of falling for marketing hype, identify the fundamentals presented in the book and repeat them over and over again. Usually, this is the closest you can get to a silver bullet.

4. Being Too Skeptical

Self-help is a polarizing genre. Some people are so skeptical of it that they consider every single piece of advice ludicrous, while others believe that every single piece of advice is life-changing. Both of these extremes are dangerous. Let's talk about skepticism first, and then we'll address naivety.

When you travel through the self-help world, skepticism is reasonable and necessary. Charlatans and opportunists abound in any industry where people are desperate for solutions. Self-improvement is no different—some authors are unscrupulous, willing to squeeze every last penny from their desperate readers by promising mountains.

Having said that, if you take skepticism too far and suspect every self-help author to be a con artist, you won't learn anything. You'll forever question every book, every page, and every word written by anyone who dares to call themselves a self-help author, even those who deserve your attention.

This approach isn't particularly conducive to learning. You need to have at least a sliver of a belief in your teacher. That's why it's essential to select the right authors to read.

If you're skeptical, you probably value logical arguments. Whenever possible, look for books that cite scientific research, quote experts you trust, or at least present the advice in a logical, well-formed manner. This shows that the author performed solid research and is probably, in a way, a skeptic like you. Ultimately, though, the best way to figure out if an author is legitimate is to try their advice yourself.

I take the following approach: Assuming the advice doesn't pose a huge risk to my well-being or the well-being of others, I try a small scale version of whatever I find to be sensible and based on sound arguments. This applies to all types of non-fiction, not just self-help.

For example, as strange as the prospect of working in a standing position was to me at the time, when I read Kelly Starrett's book *Deskbound* on the dangers of sitting, I decided to change my lifelong habit of working in a seated position.

His arguments based on evolutionary science and body physics made sense. Moreover, there wasn't much I would lose by working in a standing position for a week or two. Within a few days, I noticed reduced tightness in my back and hips, which was one of the benefits the author mentioned in the book. Several weeks later, I couldn't imagine any other way to work than by standing.

To offer you an example from a self-help book, some of the books that helped me the most were authored by Richard Koch, a British multi-millionaire writing about the 80/20 principle (you might know it as the Pareto principle, positing that the 80% of the results comes from the 20% of the efforts).

It's a counterintuitive—and often controversial—way of thinking, but the way Richard explained how it worked and how to apply it not only in business but also in personal life made sense to me. Again, I wasn't risking much. I tested it on a small scale, obtained satisfying results, tried it again in other domains, too, and have been a follower ever since.

Let me give you a rough idea about how to test this principle safely—it's the same process that led me to become such an ardent follower. Pick one area of your life you want to simplify. Think of all the factors that impact this specific field and pinpoint the ones that have the biggest impact. Now, consider how you spend more of your resources on these elements and reduce, or eliminate, the ones that are inefficient.

I tested this principle in business by assessing my marketing activities and doubling down on the ones that had been most effective. I wouldn't lose much by disregarding the other tasks for a short period of time, and I had a lot to gain if the experiment paid off. In the end, shrinking my focus proved to deliver better results than spreading myself thin over many different projects.

In my personal life, one of the simplest experiments I did was simplifying my wardrobe. I realized that I was wearing just a small proportion of my clothes the majority of the time. So, I gave away clothes I rarely wore and decided that from that moment, I would only buy high-quality, timeless, and versatile pieces of clothing. This meant that now, I can wear most of my clothes on a regular basis. Plus, I have an aversion to shopping for clothes, so thanks to this decision I was also able to save myself a lot of anguish.

You can test any other concept in a similar way, choosing one little field and performing a small scale experiment in it.

5. Being Too Naïve

I used to be a gullible self-help reader. Sometimes my unsuspecting approach worked. And sometimes I just wasted my time, money, and energy.

It would be great if we could always be trusting and have no reason to doubt an author's intentions or the effectiveness of the methods they share. Unfortunately, I wouldn't advise that.

Not every author cares about providing the best information possible. And even those with good intentions sometimes make mistakes. They might also use dangerous sweeping generalizations that hurt readers who don't know how to adapt the advice to their unique situations.

Aside from questionable authors, you should also keep in mind that not every book will help you. Don't force yourself to read something that is impractical or bores you. If I don't get any value from the first quarter of the book, I usually return it for a refund.

We've already covered how to select the right, credible authors for you. If you have difficulty judging the quality of the information, there are a couple of additional things you can do:

1. Prioritize evergreen bestsellers—The Lindy effect is an idea that posits that the future life expectancy of an idea is proportional to its current age.[1] This means that the older an idea is, the more likely it is to survive even longer. This applies to books, too.

New releases might provide up-to-date information and examples, but you're yet to see whether they'll stand the test of time. On the other hand, bestsellers released a few decades ago that still sell to this day probably discuss concepts that are effective and timeless.

Of course, this depends on the topic: human psychology doesn't change, but the technology you might use to help you reach your goals does. Whenever possible, seek evergreen advice, and in any areas that change rapidly, remember that what's presented as a fact today might be debunked tomorrow.

2. Dip your toes—No matter how great the information sounds, don't jump into the deep end right away. Curb your enthusiasm and try things out on a small scale first. Only if it works should you move on to making bigger changes.

I remember reading a controversial blog post espousing the benefits of—and I quote—"ditching your loser friends." One reader commented on the post sharing that he followed this advice and is now lonely, as everyone turned their backs on his new arrogant self.

This is how *not* to follow the life advice you find in a book, blog post, or any other place for that matter. Leaving aside the fact that the wording of this advice could be a little more delicate, if you did want to follow it, a safer approach would be to identify a person in your surroundings who has a visible, negative impact on you and see how avoiding them makes you feel.

Incidentally, inspired by another piece of advice in a similar vein, I did cut ties with a close friend with whom interactions had often left me wondering why we were still friends. This has taught me how to be more selective in my social life without obliterating my entire social circle by arrogantly calling them a bunch of losers (side note: elitist advice telling you to drop your "loser" friends is usually a sure-fire recipe for a sad, lonely life).

3. Delegate due diligence—If your friend has changed their life thanks to a particular book, it's possible that it will change yours, too. When a book repeatedly appears on recommended book lists, it's possible that you too will find it valuable. If a person you admire cites book X as a big inspiration in their life, it's possible that it will resonate with you, too.

When in doubt, delegate due diligence to others. Consult your friends, look for carefully curated lists of the best books, try the favorite books of your favorite author or a person you admire, etc.

AVOID THE 5 MOST COMMON SELF-HELP PITFALLS: QUICK RECAP

1. The first trap of self-help is reading without taking action. Self-help works only if you do something with the advice, not by merely reading it. To make yourself more likely to act, try reading books that: address your current biggest pain, offer clear how-to advice, and deliver information in simple terms.

2. The second trap of self-help is following the wrong people. To identify the authors most likely to inspire you to act, make sure that they share the attributes you're looking for in a friend. For example, they don't paint themselves as perfect, they share your core values, and have compelling personal stories to tell.

3. The third trap of self-help is seeking secrets. There are no magic pills or revolutionary methods that will change your life overnight. Focus on applicable fundamental principles, not gimmicks designed to lure you into an endless sales funnel.

4. The fourth trap of self-help is being too skeptical. Skepticism to an extent is healthy, but if you question everything, you'll never learn anything. Select the authors most likely to offer good advice and test their ideas on a small scale. If you don't trust personal experience alone, search for books that are based on scientific research and quote established experts.

5. The fifth trap of self-help is being too naïve. To better filter the information you seek: prioritize evergreen bestsellers that have stood the test of time, try ideas on a small, safe scale first, and rely on recommendations from people you trust.

Chapter 2: Read and Act Toward a Specific, Primary Purpose

In the previous chapter, I mentioned the 80/20 principle, which states that the minority of inputs produces the majority of effects. The relationship doesn't have to be precisely 80/20; what's important is the asymmetric relationship.

A business might derive 80% of their profits from 20% of their clients, or it can be 95% from 1% of their clients. For 70% of the time, you might wear only 10% of the clothes in your wardrobe, or 95% of unpleasant social interactions in your life might come from just one of your acquaintances.

Among, say, fifteen different factors contributing to the end result, only five will have a visible impact on the outcome. Out of these five, two will be responsible for disproportionately more than the remaining three. Eventually, we're left with just the one most influential factor out of the original fifteen.

This is how you should identify your primary purpose for reading self-help. This way, you'll limit your focus to the one thing that will produce the most far-reaching effects, giving you the best bang for your buck.

Don't worry, you aren't limited to just one area of your life forever. Identify what currently matters the most, use self-help to improve this specific aspect, and, once you're satisfied with the result, move on to another objective.

Think of it as moving from one chapter of your life to another. Put the spotlight on what needs the most attention at the moment. Don't worry if you can't identify only one thing—two primary purposes are okay, too, as long as you give one of them priority over the other. Even three might be fine as long as they belong to a shared theme.

To give you a practical example, when I started my self-improvement journey, I chose to concentrate on changing my negative disposition. I had to overcome pessimism first because it's impossible to change your life for the better if you always assume the worst.

When I was satisfied with my results, I picked another problem with a disproportionate impact on my life: shyness. I knew that I wouldn't be able to accomplish as much as I wanted to in life if I lacked self-confidence and was socially awkward.

In the meantime, I also focused on my fitness. I changed my diet, lost excess weight, started exercising more often, and implemented other healthy habits. Later, I began another chapter in my life: my journey as an entrepreneur.

To be clear, none of this happened in an ideal, linear fashion. During each chapter, there was an overarching theme, but it doesn't mean that I ignored other aspects of my life—and neither should you.

Life isn't perfect, and sometimes you'll be forced to focus on other things or maybe even abruptly end one chapter to move on to a different phase of your life. You might even find yourself continuously shifting from one area of focus to another.

You don't have to share your primary purpose with anyone. In fact, it's best to keep it to yourself, as you're the one who best knows what's most important to you. Sharing your purpose with others might cloud your judgment, which can lead you to pursue goals that you think you *should* pursue but are not necessarily congruent with who you are.

Which raises the question: how do you identify this purpose?

Start From the Bottom of the Pyramid

Remember Maslow's hierarchy of needs?[2] Maslow's theory posits that humans need to satisfy a few fundamental basic needs before they can advance to the next stage and fulfill further, increasingly less fundamental needs. It's represented as a pyramid with the more primary needs at the bottom and the higher needs at the top.

At the bottom, we have physiological needs. Then there's safety, love and belonging, self-esteem, and at the top of the pyramid, self-actualization.

We can adapt this theory to identify the primary area to focus on in our own lives. This model is not perfect, but overall, going from the bottom of the pyramid to the top can help you identify the most pressing issues and learn from self-help in a more focused and productive way.

If you're reading this book, it's unlikely that you suffer from chronically unsatisfied **physiological needs**, which include: homeostasis, food, water, sleep, and shelter (I'm skipping sex as a basic physiological need on purpose as its position on the pyramid is controversial).

Let's not fool ourselves here: if you're gasping for air, oxygen is all that matters. If you're starved or thirsty, food or water is the only thing that matters. Self-help can help with a lot of things, but at this stage, I don't believe that a book can help—you need the help of a fellow human being.

Obviously, as anyone with a baby can attest, sometimes you have to keep going even with little to no sleep. Other life circumstances can also temporarily interfere with the ability to meet some of the physiological needs. However, for the purpose of our discussion, the main point here is that physiological needs are the absolute first things you should attend to in any way you can, but most certainly not through resorting to self-help literature.

Moving on to **safety**. This stage includes: personal security, emotional security, financial security, and health and well-being.

Personal security is another critical factor that self-help is unlikely to solve. If you live in a war zone, a highly dangerous neighborhood, or you live with an abusive family member, please, please find a way to escape your situation first.

If you find yourself in such circumstances, don't waste your time on self-help books. A self-help book won't defend you against an abusive partner, stop a bullet, or prevent a missile from destroying your home. It might give you some pointers on how to deal with the situation, but what would help solve the problem the most would be seeking qualified assistance and support, which is beyond the scope of this book.

There are three remaining areas of this level that we might realistically improve through self-help:

emotional security (defined as the stability of your emotional state), financial security, and health and well-being.

When I discovered the self-help world, I targeted my pessimistic nature first and then addressed shyness. Both of these areas are related to emotional security, which has a far-ranging effect on all areas of life. If you're shy, you'll struggle to get a job, grow a business, find a partner, or make friends. If you can't control your anger and snap at people for no reason, your relationships will suffer and you'll sabotage your career. A stable emotional state is thus of paramount importance for a happy, fulfilling life.

Health and well-being are also crucial needs. You can't accomplish much if you constantly feel unwell. Self-help can help you quit unhealthy habits and form new, healthy ones. It can help you avoid preventable diseases and reduce or eliminate symptoms caused by bad lifestyle choices. If you're dealing with an illness, it can help you stay resilient as you fight it. It won't replace a doctor, but your mental disposition is often crucial for recovery.

One of the best starting points for health and well-being is implementing regular physical activity in your schedule. It's a *keystone habit*, defined by bestselling author Charles Duhigg in his book *The Power of Habit* as a habit that has a ripple effect. Regular exercise doesn't only improve your physical performance, but also makes you feel happier, more self-confident, and growth-oriented.

I was once injured so badly that I could barely walk for a few weeks, and I quickly noticed that the lack of physical activity had several debilitating effects on my mental performance, including weaker willpower, an inclination toward negative thinking, and a general lack of life energy. Not meeting this crucial need reverberated throughout my everyday life.

If you don't exercise at all, you might be thinking that you feel totally fine and that I'm exaggerating. Perhaps there are some exceptions, but I've found that for most people, exercise is one of those things that once implemented as a habit makes them wonder how they could live without it. It's like quitting junk food and realizing how underpowered you were by living one sugar crash to the next.

Whenever readers ask me where to start, I suggest addressing health first. I can't stress the importance of physical activity enough. Don't get me wrong: I don't think that we should all become professional athletes. It doesn't matter if you lift weights, perform gymnastics, ride a skateboard, dance, do yoga, run, swim, climb, practice martial arts, or ride a horse. It doesn't matter if you're male or female, young or old, have limited mobility, or just aren't athletically-gifted. What matters is using exercise in a way that:

- Engages your entire body so that you can strengthen it harmoniously and reduce the negative effects of a sedentary lifestyle—This helps prevent injuries, illnesses, and a general low sense of well-being.[3]

- Makes you feel good—This includes the phenomenon of the runner's high (the release of feel-good endorphins) and its equivalents in different sports: feeling better after the workout than before you started it, even if you're exhausted. Note that physical activity that you do solely because you're *supposed to* isn't a particularly good way to exercise—you should move in a way that gives you enjoyment.

- Provides a semi-meditative experience so that you can temporarily escape the everyday worries—This has a significant impact on your mental state and can help improve problem-solving skills. One such example is swimming, where simply being in the water can help to remove distractions and make you forget about the external world, if only for an hour.

Moving on from health and well-being, the last aspect of this level of the pyramid is financial security. It seems like self-help has little to do with it, but the mindset you have toward money has a massive impact on your financial situation.

If you worry about money often, self-help literature can help you change your attitude toward finances and learn how to develop the self-discipline to produce more than you consume, achieving financial security in the process.

The next stage, **love and belonging**, includes: friendships, intimacy, and family.

Self-help books are the perfect tool to improve all of these areas. You can learn how to improve your communication skills and become a better parent, spouse, or friend.

Self-esteem, defined as self-respect and status, is in many respects, a dimension of love and belonging as it includes the relationship you have with yourself as well as the people around you.

I'd prioritize developing a good relationship with yourself before focusing on developing good relationships with others. I'm by no means a relationship expert, but one thing I've learned through my own experiences is that if you don't know how to care for your personal needs, you'll struggle to meet the needs of other people. As the airplane safety demonstration goes, put on your own mask first before you help others.

Self-actualization is at the top of the pyramid, above all other needs.

Curiously, when you browse through the self-help bestseller lists, some of the most common themes include: realizing your full potential, finding your passion, becoming more spiritual, or discovering a deeper meaning of life.

As important as they may be, I'd venture to say that focusing on these needs is—most of the time—an inefficient use of self-help. If we look through the lens of the 80/20 principle, self-actualization often has a small impact on your results compared to optimizing all of the previous needs first.

What's the point of pondering on spirituality if you can barely cover your rent?

What's the point of seeking a deeper meaning to life if you're lonely and unsatisfied with your social life?

What's the point of worrying about realizing your full potential if you're suffering from preventable health issues?

I don't mean this in a malicious way. I've been there done that myself, too. I've lost countless hours worrying about self-actualization while neglecting more basic needs that would have helped me to improve myself to a more substantial degree.

Worrying if you're doing the whole self-actualization thing right when your basic needs aren't optimized is as ridiculous as worrying where you'll store your private jet before you make your first million.

I've found that achieving self-actualization often comes as a side effect of tending to the more fundamental needs.

Need to find a deeper meaning to life? Focus on your love and belonging stage and you'll find a great reason to live.

Struggling with a lack of fulfillment? Barring clinical conditions, focus on forming healthy habits that create a positive loop for your mental state, which will then get you closer to fulfillment, too. In my case, out of all the tricks I tried to overcome my recurring depressive tendencies, the most effective one was simply exercising, particularly outdoors.

Of course, if you consider spirituality a basic need in your life, then you should by all means actively focus on that stage as well. Having said that, I'd still argue that addressing all of your basic needs first will help you accomplish your spiritual goals more than reading books on how to achieve enlightenment would. As the Zen Buddhist saying goes, "Before enlightenment, chop wood, carry water. After enlightenment, chop wood, carry water."

When in Doubt, Pick From Any of These

If you're still unsure of what goal to focus on first, here are five of the most transformational objectives that self-help can assist you in achieving.

1. **Getting in shape**—As we've already established, health is essential for any life pursuit. Whether it's losing weight, exercising more, quitting bad habits or forming new healthy ones, any of these can change your life dramatically.

2. **Optimizing your career and finances**—Self-help can help you advance your career, rebrand yourself, become an entrepreneur, or fix your financial situation by learning how to be more disciplined with money. All of this can bring dramatic life change, too.

3. Optimizing your relationships—Finding a significant other, starting a family, becoming a better spouse, and other pursuits related to relationships have a big impact on your life satisfaction, if not the biggest (following health).

4. Becoming a better student—By this, I mean learning skills and developing traits that will give you more opportunities in life. This includes developing your self-confidence, a strong work ethic, public speaking skills, etc.

5. Changing your lifestyle—Self-help can help you figure out how to follow your dreams, stop working to please others and focus on what you truly want, or start a new chapter in life. This includes: traveling the world, moving to your dream location, transitioning into retirement, gaining confidence to quit a job you hate to pursue something more exciting, etc.

Okay, But How Do I Actually Put This Into Practice?

Follow these steps:

1. Create a mind map or make a list with the most important factors affecting the specific problem you want to solve. For example, if you want to get in shape, you might list: overcoming the temptation to eat junk food, being too lazy to exercise, or struggling to prepare healthy meals.

2. Filter the books you want to read according to how effective you think they will be at helping you deal with these specific issues. Read free samples, take a look at the table of contents, and read reviews.

3. Read the chosen books and apply the advice they offer through the lens of the specific area you're focused on now. For example, if you want to become more assertive at work, think how you can follow the recommendations from the books in specific situations you encounter regularly at the office.

4. Don't move on to another book until you've acted on the book you're currently reading (unless it turns out to be a bad book). Even if you manage to implement only one piece of advice, it still puts you one step closer to fixing your current biggest problem.

5. Resist the temptation to read books on a different topic until you're satisfied with the improvement in your chosen area of focus.

READ AND ACT TOWARD A SPECIFIC, PRIMARY PURPOSE: QUICK RECAP

1. To learn from self-help more efficiently, identify your primary purpose for reading it. It should be an important aspect of your life that has lasting, far-reaching effects. This way, instead of reading for the sake of reading, you'll read for a specific reason tied to an important area of your life you'd like to improve.

2. Use Maslow's pyramid to identify any needs in your life that you repeatedly fail to satisfy. By moving in stages from the bottom of the pyramid up, you'll always focus on what currently has the potential to improve your life the most.

3. Self-help won't help you address your most basic needs. Seek qualified help when you're dealing with constant hunger, danger to your life, or any situation that prevents you from feeling secure and meeting your most basic bodily needs.

4. Self-actualization is one of the most common topics in self-help, yet it's the one area that you can ignore for a long time, if not altogether. Focusing on

the lower needs that can have a more significant impact often helps you meet your self-actualization needs, too.

5. Five key areas of life that you can focus on to bring about dramatic change are: getting in shape, optimizing your career and finances, optimizing your relationships, becoming a better student, and implementing dramatic lifestyle changes like moving to a different place.

6. To put the idea of primary purpose into practice, break down your specific area of focus into smaller challenges and then find books that would be most helpful to address these challenges. When reading, keep these specific problems in mind— always remember your primary purpose, don't read just for the sake of it. Don't move on to another book until you apply something from the one you're currently reading.

Chapter 3: Explore Different Perspectives

Confirmation bias is the tendency to seek information that confirms your beliefs. It also makes you remember facts selectively or interpret information that you don't agree with in a biased way.[4]

People who succumb to this bias find themselves stuck in the status quo. They live in a bubble, protecting themselves from different perspectives even if their current beliefs don't serve them well.

I know this trap firsthand and was stuck in a confirmation bias loop for years, refusing to accept new information relating to my fitness goals.

When I started lifting weights, I became attached to the idea that the most effective bodybuilding approach was to focus on just a few compound exercises, including squats, deadlifts, and bench presses. I quickly accepted this as true and closed my mind to different perspectives on exercise. Nothing else would help me achieve my fitness goals besides this specific training method.

I followed this method religiously for a couple of years, refusing to learn about other approaches. While it did somewhat help me, my results were lackluster compared to what I was promised by bodybuilding gurus.

I wanted to try other approaches like calisthenics (bodyweight exercises), but I was too uncomfortable with the idea of contradicting my beliefs. After all, I was following the only correct approach there was, right? Even when I searched for information about calisthenics, I subconsciously looked for arguments against it, just so I could "prove myself right."

Eventually, I grew to hate lifting weights. Each session left me feeling worse at the end than when I started. Instead of feeling fit, strong, and limber, I felt heavy, slow, and tense. Even then, when it was beyond evident that this fitness approach didn't serve me well, it still took me several months to open my mind to new perspectives. Eventually, I started experimenting with other sports. I discovered rock climbing, flirted with different types of physical activities, and finally turned my approach to fitness on its head.

Today, I prioritize holistic fitness and growth. I still perform strength workouts, but I no longer lift weights. Instead, I work with my body weight through a variety of calisthenic exercises and yoga that not only make me stronger but also more agile. I focus more on the health and optimal performance of my entire body rather than a specific part or muscle mass, as is often the case with traditional bodybuilding.

I'm not saying that lifting weights is a waste of time. It works for many people. It just didn't work for me. Of course, we could argue that I exercised with poor form, had an improper diet, or otherwise made mistakes that prevented me from getting the results I was after. Still, this wouldn't change the fact that what I do now, the approach that contradicted my earlier beliefs, is more aligned with my preferences and lifestyle.

I found something that works for me, and if you're doing something that works for you, we're both happy. What I want to communicate through sharing my fitness story is how dangerous the confirmation bias is and how stubborn we can be about our beliefs, even if they sabotage our results.

Now, you might recall that I recommended finding authors who are similar to you. But wouldn't this be an example of closing your mind to other perspectives? Indeed, it is. However, there's a point to it.

If you're stuck in a rut of reading without taking action, it's important to start by limiting yourself to the perspective that most closely matches your own. This way, you'll be more likely to take action. Once you break the loop of reading without doing, you're ready to broaden your horizons and explore other perspectives. But again, the first thing you need to do is to train yourself to take action—and the most effective way to do so is by reducing confusion and picking just one point of view to follow.

For example, I used to follow a strict school of self-discipline. I thought that if you wanted to be disciplined, you had to suck it up and be tough. I used to be less understanding of the flaws we all have. I was more critical toward myself and others and, by extension, less empathetic to others and out of tune with both the world around and within myself.

I won't say that the strict approach is bad. I sought the advice of people espousing the merits of mental toughness because that's what I considered closest to my beliefs back then. And as a result, that was how I was able to consistently act on what I learned and obtain results.

At one point, however, I grew tired of always being so tough on myself. The strict school of thought served its purpose, and I opened myself to new perspectives that emphasized sustainability.

I haven't abandoned the old school of thought completely. I still subject myself to stress occasionally, but I now do it more consciously, with an emphasis on the long-term outlook.

Your journey with self-improvement will require a similarly fluid approach. We all evolve. What worked at one point might stop working later on. What you believed to be the best approach might morph into something new that employs strategies you didn't agree with before.

It doesn't mean that you should continuously shift from one approach to another, always in pursuit of the next shiny thing. Remember that immediate results are rare, even with the most viable strategies. It pays to stick things out to see if they have an effect before you dump them. When something works well for you, be faithful. When you feel you're ready for something else, open yourself to different perspectives.

An open mind is an essential tool for continuous self-improvement. In the rest of this chapter, we'll cover some methods to help you explore different perspectives.

Run Experiments

Running small scale experiments is an excellent way to employ new points of view.

Choose an idea you want to test. Decide how long you plan to run the experiment. Depending on the idea, anywhere from a few days to a few weeks could be optimal. Establish a metric that will help you judge how effective the idea is, such as your subjective well-being on a scale from 1 to 10 or tangible results related to your goal (profits, body weight, strength, blood tests, etc.).

Whenever possible, test different approaches one after another so you can compare which one works best for you.

If you want to lose weight, you can test a restrictive approach for a month and then, for comparison, test an approach that lets you indulge in scheduled cheat meals. This way, you'll discover through your own experience whether you do better completely abstaining from temptations or allowing them in moderation.

If you want to become more productive, you can first test a time management method that organizes your day (like the advice David Allen offers in his book *Getting Things Done*). Then you can test its complete opposite in which you disregard every single task except the most important one (like Gary Keller suggests in his book *The One Thing*).

Don't be afraid to test even the most sacred concepts of self-help, such as waking up early. I'm a huge proponent of waking up early, but I formed my opinion through personal experience and not just because it's considered a habit of the successful. I used to be a night owl. When compared to my old routine, my early bird life works better for me, and I can't imagine it any other way. For you, it might be the other way around—that's something you can only discover through testing both approaches.

You can test other ideas that don't require dramatic, irreversible changes to your life in the same way.

Combine Both Approaches

We like to think in binary terms. There's black and white. The weather is good or bad. He's wrong and she's right. You're with us or against us. Yes or no.

Sometimes binary thinking is useful. If you're about to hit a tree, it's better to choose between swerving left or right instead of pondering different possibilities.

Dangerous situations aside, when we engage in black-and-white thinking, we pigeonhole ourselves in a self-engineered cage. We forget that self-improvement is not an exact science. It relies on personal experience, not laws of physics. One of the trickiest things about self-help is that it's highly subjective, with different methods working for different people.

You can't put a thousand volunteers in a lab, tell them which self-help concepts to follow, and compare which group became more successful five years later. In fact, you can't even compare two successful people. Two professional athletes follow different training protocols. Two billionaires build their wealth in different industries and through different means. Two widely-acclaimed painters paint in contrasting styles.

When it comes to self-help, forget about black and white. Forget about right and wrong. Forget about there being only two extremes with nothing in between. Consider combining two different approaches by taking some ideas from one and some ideas from its polar opposite. Here are a few of my personal examples:

1. I believe that **procrastination is a good thing** because it tells you that whatever you're putting off is something you don't want to do. Usually, if you postpone something, it's because it's boring, frustrating, painful, or otherwise disagrees with you. Consequently, instead of forcing myself to do the tasks I put off, I question whether to engage in them at all, as they might be a bad use of my resources.

But there are countless shades between black and white. Sometimes you have an off day and procrastinate on everything, including tasks that do matter or that you usually enjoy. Then there are some tasks that we dislike but can't eliminate or outsource. Lastly, there are some tasks that make us feel uncomfortable but are the very ones we should perform to change our lives.

Therefore, I don't always automatically assume that every task I put off is unnecessary. For the best results, you sometimes have to shift your perspective to its polar opposite. In this case, it would mean viewing procrastination not as your friend, but as your enemy. For me, the most important lesson this perspective offers is that you can reduce resistance through momentum.

Whenever I catch myself postponing a task that I *should* engage in, I focus on one low-effort task I can perform to get started. For example, when I don't feel like cleaning the house, I start with something easy like sweeping the floor in just one room. More often than not, taking one tiny action leads to another. Before I know it, I'm halfway through the difficult task.

2. **I don't believe in inspiring yourself to take action by watching inspirational speeches or videos**. If you need to watch a Rocky clip to motivate yourself to go to the gym, you should reconsider your

internal motivators rather than rely on a motivational speech.

I stay away from inspirational content and try my best not to sound "inspirational" in my books. I associate "inspiration" with people who fool themselves into thinking they're taking action just because they've watched an inspirational video (I'm not singling you out, I once believed in this stuff, too).

But my perspective is just one of many different points of view. I have an aversion to banal inspirational messages, but I do agree that having a positive mental state can push you to take action. I don't watch inspirational videos when I feel down, but I do engage in other activities to lift my spirits and inspire me to take action.

This way, I combine different perspectives. I value engaging in habits religiously even when you don't feel like doing so, but I also understand that on a bad day, sometimes you need a little boost to help you keep going.

3. **I enjoy periodically subjecting myself to some extreme experiments and testing out unconventional approaches**. Tell me a common way of doing something and I'll be looking for outliers and a contrarian approach.

I appreciate a non-conformist attitude because, *in my opinion*, extraordinary results usually require extraordinary measures. It's also plain fun to try unconventional ideas.

At the same time, I don't do eccentric things for the sake of being eccentric. Some conventional approaches are more sensible than non-traditional ones. Sometimes the weird ideas don't work well in everyday life or work only for a small group of people under specific circumstances.

Striking a balance between the conventional and the unusual is taking the best of two extremes. Nobody said that you have to blindly follow only one perspective. No matter how uncommon it is, there's no point in wearing pants backwards. Likewise, there's no point in doing everything in the exact same way as the Joneses, either.

Become a Beginner Again

Sometimes the best way to move forward is by taking a big step back.

When I started learning how to surf, I took a few classes from instructors who specialized primarily in teaching tourists who wanted to catch one wave and cross surfing off their bucket lists (again, there's nothing wrong with that).

Consequently, the instructors' focus wasn't on teaching the proper technique, etiquette, and safety. They were focused on helping their clients catch a wave at all costs—an approach that does help accomplish this specific goal, but little else beyond it (such as teaching tourists how to be safe in the ocean).

When I traveled to another destination and hired another instructor to help me progress, he wasn't happy with what those instructors had taught me. He didn't care about me catching waves for the sake of catching them—he wanted to teach me how to understand the ocean and learn proper technique and attitude, not just push me into the waves.

He asked me to forget everything I had been taught so that we could start with a blank slate. I had to discard what I had learned to become a complete beginner again and open myself to a new perspective.

Sometimes becoming a beginner again is the only sensible approach. If you've built your knowledge on the wrong fundamentals, it's more beneficial to pretend you'd never learned any of it and start anew without any preconceived notions. It's humbling to become a newbie in something you have experience with, but relearning might be the very thing you need to accomplish your goals.

One of my favorite quotes is that of Zen Buddhist teacher Shunryū Suzuki, who said: "in the beginner's mind there are many possibilities, in the expert's mind there are few."[5]

Don't be afraid to become a beginner again. Or better yet, never become an expert—refer to yourself as a lifelong student always open to new ideas, even if they're in conflict with what you've been taught.

EXPLORE DIFFERENT PERSPECTIVES: QUICK RECAP

1. Because of confirmation bias, a tendency to seek information that confirms your beliefs, you often close your mind to new perspectives that might provide better results than the approach you currently follow. Consequently, it's important to learn how to expose yourself to new points of view.

2. One of the ways to explore different perspectives is to run experiments. Pick two different approaches and test them one after another to identify which works best for you. This way, you form opinions based on your own experience and real-world results over merely reading.

3. Another idea to open your mind and accomplish more is to combine polar opposite ideas. Examine the different approaches individually and think about how you can harness the best of both of them.

4. Sometimes the only way to move forward is to forget everything you've learned and become a beginner again. Or better yet, don't ever refer to

yourself as an expert—assume that there's always more to learn and that you'll never master any given domain.

Chapter 4: Self-Improvement Is About the Self

In an interview for the book *Tribe of Mentors* by Tim Ferriss, when asked about advice he would give to a smart, driven college student, billionaire philanthropist John Arnold said:

"For every entrepreneur who thrived by resolutely working on a singular idea for many years, there is another who pivoted wildly. For every successful individual who designed a master plan for life, there is another who was deliberately spontaneous. Ignore advice, especially early in one's career. There is no universal path to success."[6]

Ultimately, we all have to blaze our own paths. We can't follow somebody's footsteps and expect to land in the exact same place. Every person has different goals, likes and dislikes, values, beliefs, and opinions and lives under different circumstances.

Copying someone's approach to a T makes sense if we're talking about specific skill sets, particularly those with potentially catastrophic consequences. You don't blaze your own path as a surgeon or a commercial pilot—you learn how it's done and definitely *don't* ignore the advice given to you by experienced surgeons or pilots.

But personal development is different because, as the name implies, it's all *personal*. Self-help books can teach you ways to improve yourself. What you can't outsource, though, is executing these ideas. And to do so, you need to interpret these ideas for your specific circumstances.

Turn Data Into Information

No matter how specific and easily digestible the advice you acquire from a self-help book is, I like to think of it more like *data*—bits of information—than actual *information,* defined as *interpreted* data.

To turn data from self-help books into information, you need to interpret it in a way that takes into account the reality that you're a living, breathing thing, not a robot that always responds to the commands in the exact same way.

For example, in some of my books, I recommend taking cold showers to build the ability to withstand discomfort. By itself, it's just data. To make it useful, you need to ask yourself if it's something that will help you. Of course, you can go try it right now—this would be the simplest way to judge its effectiveness for you. But some concepts require more investment on your part, and even if they don't, considering your internal wiring and specific circumstances helps you decide which ideas can actually work, and which you can skip.

Continuing with the cold showers example, what's your experience with pushing your limits? A soldier or an adventure junkie probably doesn't need cold showers to get tougher—they've already experienced worse things that have stretched their comfort zones.

What specific goal are you focused on right now? Would taking cold showers help accomplish it? If you need to get tougher because you want to join the army, cold showers might help. If your primary goal is to reduce stress, then perhaps cold showers aren't the best idea right now.

Then there are other personal factors. Maybe you tolerate the cold well. Maybe you hate living in your cold city and don't want to be cold inside your home as well as out. Maybe you have a medical condition that prevents you from taking cold showers. Or maybe you simply hate the idea and don't understand how taking cold showers would be useful to anyone except masochists.

These are all valid reasons to discard this idea—after all, we're looking for something that will work well for *you*. You shouldn't feel forced to try every single idea you encounter, particularly when your gut is against it.

Cold showers are not a prerequisite to success—it's just one of the countless ideas that can help you grow your comfort zone, but doesn't necessarily have to be the right one for you.

Discover why you're drawn toward certain ideas and opposed to others, and you'll better understand your beliefs, values, strengths, and weaknesses. This knowledge will then help you identify the authors, books, concepts, and specific tips that will aid you the most.

You can take this process further and similarly examine yourself when you accomplish your goals, or when you're undecided about whether to keep pursuing them.

For example, one of my goals was to learn skydiving. I completed the theory course, jumped twice, and decided against pursuing it further even though I paid for three jumps in advance. I'd call myself something of a risk-taker, but upon analyzing the risk and reward ratio, I decided that for me personally, the risks weren't worth the rewards.

I'm not going to pretend otherwise: I was deathly afraid of another jump (which is a great understatement), and I understood that I went well past my risk tolerance. Deep in my gut, I knew it was time to back off.

Whenever you accomplish a goal that doesn't leave you fulfilled, or worse, makes you regret pursuing it, ask yourself why and in which direction you want to grow next, having established that the previous path wasn't the right one for you. For this, you need to seek answers within—nobody knows you better than you do. Which leads us to the practice of introspection.

A Practice to Consider: Seek Answers Within

There are hundreds upon hundreds of resources that can help you with every single aspect of life from self-discipline to mindfulness, dieting to spirituality, relationships to creativity.

The standard approach to solving a problem is to grab the first internet device within your reach, open the search engine of your choice, and type in whatever you're struggling with. Then we spend hours consulting other people: reading their books, watching their videos, listening to their podcasts, or skimming their blog posts. Occasionally we even pay for their time, hoping that a 60-minute consultation will give us all the answers.

Sometimes other people *do* know what's best for you. A drug addict believes that drugs are good for them; their friends and family know better. A morbidly obese person believes that eating ten cheeseburgers a day isn't that unhealthy; a doctor who knows their blood pressure tells a different thing. A student thinks that they've mastered a particular skill; a teacher knows they aren't even close.

But when it comes to personal challenges, nobody will understand you better than you, and nobody will give you better answers than the answers you'll find in yourself.

As we constantly seek external answers to solve every challenge in our lives, we lose the ability to solve these problems ourselves. We stop thinking for ourselves and instead delegate thinking to others.

There's a lot we can learn from other people, but sometimes the only way to overcome a personal challenge is to disregard everything you've researched and work through the problem yourself. Journal, brainstorm possible solutions, or just stare at a piece of paper until something comes up.

If you're easily distracted, book a session in a sensory deprivation tank. It's essentially a giant bathtub with a lid that temporarily takes your sensory abilities away. It's soundproof, lightless, and filled with salt water at skin temperature. There's so much salt inside that you float, which is why these tanks are sometimes called float tanks.

The point of putting yourself through this claustrophobic, psychedelic experience is that you're in there by yourself, without any distractions. Few places are more conducive to self-introspection than float tanks.

Meditating at home with noise canceling headphones on or taking a walk in the wilderness, away from other people and without phone reception, is helpful, too.

Yes, doing what appears to be nothing will be frustrating. But in fact, you'll be engaged in one of the most important things you can do for yourself: applying your own experiences to solving your own problem in a way that's unique and tailored to you;

something that no external resource can help you accomplish.

What You Can and Cannot Learn From Self-Help—a Handy, Non-Exhaustive List

1. You can learn what science says about the psychology of willpower. You can't learn which particular strategies will work best for you.

2. You can learn what a successful entrepreneur did to build his or her company. You can't learn every single step you'll have to take to build your own business.

3. You can learn how an acclaimed athlete keeps going when his or her body breaks down. You can't learn how to inspire yourself to persevere when your body starts shutting down.

4. You can learn about the morning routine of a motivational speaker. You can't learn what type of routine will work best for you (it might not even be a morning routine, but an evening one).

5. You can learn the most effective strategies to keep distractions at bay. You can't learn what types

of distractions impact you the most and how you should personally deal with them.

6. You can learn how to have a healthy diet, be active, and sleep well. You can't learn what type of healthy foods you'll find the most optimal for you, what type of physical exercise will make you look forward to doing it, or how you need to structure your lifestyle to ensure a good night's sleep.

7. You can learn from this book how to help yourself with self-help. You can't learn which specific books, concepts, and people will have the largest impact on your life.

How can you learn all of the things you *can't* learn from reading?

By putting aside the books and figuring things out yourself. By asking yourself questions, trying different things, and failing your way to success.

Ultimately, as the title of this chapter indicates, you can't take the "self" out of self-improvement. It all starts and ends with you and the work you need to perform yourself to accomplish your goals.

SELF-IMPROVEMENT IS ABOUT THE SELF: QUICK RECAP

1. There are no universal paths to success. To make self-help work for you, you need to take into account your own goals, values, likes and dislikes, beliefs, circumstances, etc.

2. The ideas you get from self-help books are more like raw data than information. To make it valuable for you, you need to interpret it in a way that reflects who you are.

3. The best answers come from within. Periodically engage in self-introspective sessions in a quiet, distraction-free place where you can dive into your mind to figure out how to overcome your challenges and move forward.

4. Self-improvement literature can tell you what somebody else is doing, but it won't tell you what will work specifically for you. This job is yours and yours only—there's a reason why we call it *self-*improvement.

Chapter 5: Go Beyond Traditional Self-Help

In the same way that you don't value the tenth free slice of pizza as much as the first one (unless you really, really love pizza), the law of diminishing marginal utility applies to self-help books, too.

Read five self-help classics, and you'll come away inspired by all the new ideas. Read another five, and then another five, and you'll eventually have déjà vu as the same ideas reappear over and over again.

After failing to learn anything new from another book, you might even decide that it's time to stop reading self-help. But self-help doesn't consist only of those garden-variety books. While it makes sense to focus on them in the beginning, eventually, when you've read all the classics, it's time to fine-tune your approach. In this chapter, we'll cover several ways to do so.

Go Deeper and More Specific

Books that focus exclusively on a narrow topic or a specific problem will often offer more valuable advice than more general titles.

For example, let's imagine that you want to start exercising regularly. You can read a generic self-help book on how to build habits. This might help you form the habit of regular exercise, but there will be many blanks the book won't fill.

There are many unique challenges associated with exercise than a generic book on habits won't address. For example, how do you form an exercise habit if you're strapped for time, so out of shape that you can barely climb a set of stairs, or dealing with other challenges you aren't sure how to solve? That's when it's better to find a book that's more specific, especially if it's written by an expert on one particular topic.

Sometimes you can go even deeper and **find a book that addresses a specific audience**. For example, you can find books that discuss how to form an exercise habit if you're a busy mother, if you're over 60, or if you're disabled. Forming such a habit will come with different challenges depending on your circumstances.

You'll be more prepared and more likely to take action when you read a book that addresses your specific pain points and gives you ideas about how to solve them. A teenager won't face the same challenges as a retiree.

Another way to go deeper and more specific is to **find books written by people who excel in the area you want to master**, though not necessarily in other areas. Many self-help books are written by generalists. They might still offer good advice, but it likely won't help you as much as learning from a specialist.

For example, you can learn how to stay resilient from a general book on mental toughness. However, if you want to become a mountaineer, you'll learn more from a book written by one, sharing their real-world experience of how they keep going despite adverse conditions such as dangerous weather, strife within the team, or utter mental and physical exhaustion.

Such a mountaineer will give you the best advice regarding mental toughness in the highly specific skill of mountaineering, but they might not give you accurate advice on how to persevere when building a business—for that, you'll need to find an accomplished entrepreneur who's been in those trenches.

Sometimes It's Better to Skip Self-Help

Self-help isn't the only genre that can help you improve yourself. Any book can have a lasting impact on your life, but there are a few genres in particular that can change your life outside of the obvious. Consider the following alternatives:

1. Read Autobiographies and Biographies

By far, one of the best genres to transition into after you get tired of self-help is autobiographies and biographies.

If the author is a person you admire, there's nothing better—short of a real-world conversation—

to learn their story, understand how they think, and implement their ideas in your own life.

I prefer autobiographies over biographies. In the case of the latter, it's the biographer who chooses how to portray and interpret the story of the subject. Still, a well-written biography can be helpful to better understand those you admire.

2. Read History Books and Books Written a Long Time Ago

History books rarely come with clear-cut conclusions on how to improve your life. It's the reader's interpretation that makes them useful (or not).

It pays to learn from the pioneers of a domain you'd like to master, seek information about how people lived in the ancient times, or read about how our ancestors survived adverse conditions.

Books written a long time ago, having stood the test of time, are some of the most valuable books you can ever read. Granted, not all of them, but the vast majority are considered classics to this day for a reason. People have found them valuable ever since they were published. Throughout different ages, they have influenced those who have read them, and so they were kept alive by virtue of their intrinsic, timeless value.

When you think about it, isn't it miraculous that we can learn from people who lived a hundred, a thousand, or even a few thousand years ago?

Ancient Stoic philosopher Seneca the Younger wrote in the year 49 AD in his essay *On the Shortness of Life*:[7]

"Of all people only those are at leisure who make time for philosophy, only those are really alive. For they not only keep a good watch over their own lifetimes, but they annex every age to theirs. All the years that have passed before them are added to their own.

(…)

Since nature allows us to enter into a partnership with every age, why not turn from this brief and transient spell of time and give ourselves wholeheartedly to the past, which is limitless and eternal and can be shared with better men than we?"

Better men—and women—who lived before us gave us an extraordinary, timeless gift by sharing their perspectives and often faced the exact same problems we're dealing with today. Why not explore their minds?

3. Read Books Pertinent to Your Interests

We shouldn't define personal development as an area limited to the topics most commonly discussed in self-help books like mindset, self-discipline, or habits. The ultimate goal is to *improve yourself*. We can improve in countless ways, not just through forming new habits.

No matter what your passion or area of expertise is, broadening your knowledge in it makes you a better person. Often, investing in specific skills that have nothing to do with traditional self-help topics is a better use of your resources than reading yet another generic advice book.

For example, a musician whose music gives joy to thousands of people can arguably improve themselves more by studying music theory than by reading a book on the mindset of successful people.

One of my current interests is expanding my knowledge about the perils of a sedentary lifestyle and how to counteract its adverse effects (side note: almost all of us are sedentary—even if you exercise a few hours a week, what do you do with the remaining time?).

I want to understand what movements are most natural to human beings and how we can structure our everyday lives to reflect our natural habitat (here's a hint: it's not a dark office in an air-conditioned building) to be healthier. This topic has little to do with self-help, but since I currently have only a basic understanding of it, I'm learning a lot more than by reading another generic self-help book.

Whatever your interests are, strive to constantly expand your knowledge. It doesn't matter how irrelevant the topic is to the general public—what matters is that you enjoy studying it and that there at least *some* people who are also interested in it and can benefit from your education.

4. Read About Something You Have No Knowledge About

I recently read a book on freediving—something I was clueless about prior to reading the book (if you're curious, it was *Deep: Freediving, Renegade Science, and What the Ocean Tells Us about Ourselves* by James Nestor).

I not only learned that the human limits are farther than I thought (can you believe that the best freedivers can dive on a single breath for up to *nine minutes*?). I also discovered a fascinating world of people pushing their limits and science forward, helping the environment, and, in the process, becoming better individuals.

The lessons you gain from reading books about topics you know nothing about aren't always easily applicable to your life. However, I've found that there's always a way to draw some parallels between a foreign domain and a domain you're familiar with. For example, the freediving book stressed the importance of meticulous preparation (you can't just jump into the water and dive into the depths), which is something I could improve in myself—not for freediving, but for other aspects of my life.

Broadening your horizons makes you a better student of life. And who knows, maybe you'll end up developing a passion for a new topic.

5. Read Fiction

Human beings are wired for stories. Arguably, most of human progress has been driven largely by stories. We use stories to pass lessons from one generation to another. We use stories to rally people behind a common cause. Stories resonate on a deep, emotional level that a how-to book can't match.

The structure of a story relies on conflict and resolution, depicting how a character overcomes obstacles and keeps going, growing through the process.

Furthermore, according to various studies, reading fiction stimulates our brains and helps develop empathy and social skills.[8] It has been shown to bring deep relaxation and inner calm. People who read fiction regularly sleep better, have lower stress levels, enjoy higher self-esteem, and experience lower rates of depression than non-readers.[9] In a way, literature makes us better human beings.

Don't discount the benefits of reading fiction. Rest is as important as work. There's nothing wrong in reading fiction for pleasure, to forget about your worries and recharge your batteries.

GO BEYOND TRADITIONAL SELF-HELP: QUICK RECAP

1. For advice more tailored to your unique challenges, find titles that discuss a specific aspect of a certain problem instead of just the general concept. For example, look for a book on how to build an exercise habit rather than how to build a habit in general. Whenever possible, look for a book written specifically for an audience to which you belong, such as a book written for middle-age female entrepreneurs. For laser-focused advice, find books written by masters in their chosen fields instead of those written by generalists.

2. Self-help isn't the only genre that can help you improve yourself. You can also learn a lot from autobiographies and biographies of people you admire.

3. History is another genre that can teach you a lot. You will not only expand your general knowledge of the subject you're studying but also learn from the mistakes and successes of people from the past. Consider reading books written a long time ago,

too—our ancestors faced many of the same problems we face today, and their different perspectives might help you more than a modern take on the subject.

4. Personal development is about bettering yourself in all aspects of life, not just the commonly discussed self-help topics like mindset. This means that instead of reading another self-help book, you can also improve yourself by studying what interests you and continuously expanding your knowledge.

5. Sometimes you can draw surprisingly useful conclusions from a book on a topic you don't know much about. For example, even if you don't plan to become a freediver, the lessons about the human limits those individuals push can help you attain your own goals.

6. Human beings are wired for stories. We learn from them, draw inspiration from them, and escape to them to forget about the real world. Don't discount the benefits of fiction, even if just as a way to recharge your batteries.

Epilogue

Self-help is useless.

Self-help is life-changing.

Which one will it be for you?

The answer lies in your hands. Or, more precisely, in what books you hold in them and whether you limit yourself to merely reading those books or use them as tools to take action.

We discussed how to avoid common traps, how to find the right books for you, how to keep your mind open to new perspectives, and how to turn theoretical advice into real-world information you can use to better your life.

If there's just one thing to remember from this book, let it be this: please, please don't make the mistake of equating reading with personal growth. A book can provide ideas and inspiration, but you'll always get better results by *doing* than reading.

Self-help literature is just one aspect of self-improvement. There are people who have read countless self-help books but failed to act on any of them. There are also people who have never read a single self-help book yet constantly push forward, becoming better versions of themselves.

You don't have to always read new books. There's no rule saying that if you don't read the classic self-help bestsellers, you'll never become successful, or if you don't read new releases, you'll be left behind.

Remember: there are no secrets. In the end, it all comes back to gaining fundamental knowledge and applying it over and over again, tweaking your approach and tailoring it to your needs.

Download Another Book for Free

I want to thank you for buying my book and offer you another book (just as valuable as this one): *Grit: How to Keep Going When You Want to Give Up*, completely free.

Visit the link below to receive it:

https://www.profoundselfimprovement.com/selfhelp

In *Grit*, I'll tell you exactly how to stick to your goals, using proven methods from peak performers and science.

In addition to getting *Grit*, you'll also have an opportunity to get my new books for free, enter giveaways, and receive other valuable emails from me.

Again, here's the link to sign up:

https://www.profoundselfimprovement.com/selfhelp

Could You Help?

I'd love to hear your opinion about my book. In the world of book publishing, there are few things more valuable than honest reviews from a wide variety of readers.

Your review will help other readers find out whether my book is for them. It will also help me reach more readers by increasing the visibility of my book.

About Martin Meadows

Martin Meadows is a bestselling personal development author, writing about self-discipline and its transformative power to help you become successful and live a more fulfilling life. With a straight-to-the-point approach, he is passionate about sharing tips, habits, and resources for self-improvement through a combination of science-backed research and personal experience.

Embracing self-control helped Martin overcome extreme shyness, build successful businesses, learn multiple languages, become a bestselling author, and more. As a lifelong learner, he enjoys exploring the limits of his comfort zone through often extreme experiments and adventures involving various sports and wild or exotic places.

Martin uses a pen name. It helps him focus on serving the readers through writing, without the distractions of seeking recognition. He doesn't believe in branding himself as an infallible expert (which he is not), opting instead to offer suggestions and solutions as a fellow personal growth experimenter, with all of the associated failures and successes.

You can read his books here:

http://www.amazon.com/author/martinmeadows.

[1] Taleb, N. (2012). *Antifragile: Things That Gain from Disorder*. Random House.

[2] Maslow, A.H. (1943). A theory of human motivation. *Psychological Review*. 50(4): 370–96. doi:10.1037/h0054346.

[3] Cooney, G. M., Dwan, K., Greig, C. A., Lawlor, D. A., Rimer, J., Waugh, F. R., McMurdo, M., Mead, G. E. (2013). Exercise for depression. *Cochrane Database of Systematic Reviews*. 12 September 2013. doi: 10.1002/14651858.CD004366.pub6.

[4] Plous, S. (1993).*The Psychology of Judgment and Decision Making*. McGraw-Hill.

[5] *Suzuki, S. (1970). Zen Mind, Beginner's Mind. Weatherhill.*

[6] Ferriss, T. (2017). *Tribe of Mentors*. Houghton Mifflin Harcourt.

[7] Seneca the Younger (49 AD). De Brevitate Vitae (On the Shortness of Life).

[8] Paul, A. M. (2012, March 17). The Neuroscience of Your Brain on Fiction. Retrieved April 4, 2019, from https://www.nytimes.com/2012/03/18/opinion/sunday/the-neuroscience-of-your-brain-on-fiction.html?pagewanted=all.

[9] Dovey, C. (2018, July 17). Can Reading Make You Happier? Retrieved April 4, 2019, from https://www.newyorker.com/culture/cultural-comment/can-reading-make-you-happier.